Designed by Nature

Transportation Technology

Wendy Hinote Lanier
and John Willis

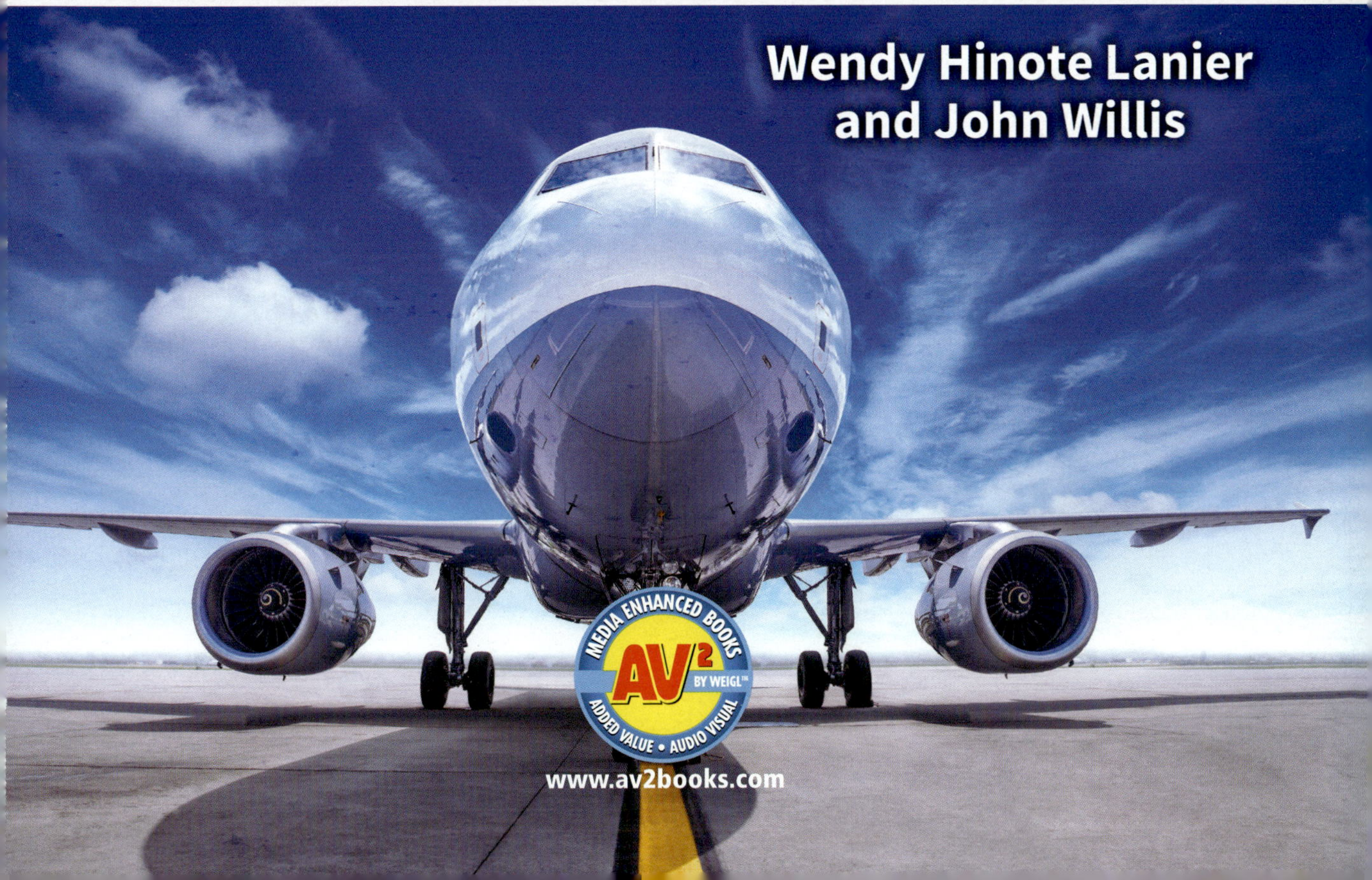

MEDIA ENHANCED BOOKS
AV2 BY WEIGL
ADDED VALUE • AUDIO VISUAL
www.av2books.com

Go to www.av2books.com, and enter this book's unique code.

BOOK CODE

AVX76442

AV² by Weigl brings you media enhanced books that support active learning.

AV² provides enriched content that supplements and complements this book. Weigl's AV² books strive to create inspired learning and engage young minds in a total learning experience.

Your AV² Media Enhanced books come alive with...

Audio
Listen to sections of the book read aloud.

Video
Watch informative video clips.

Embedded Weblinks
Gain additional information for research.

Try This!
Complete activities and hands-on experiments.

Key Words
Study vocabulary, and complete a matching word activity.

Quizzes
Test your knowledge.

Slide Show
View images and captions, and prepare a presentation.

... and much, much more!

Published by AV² by Weigl
350 5th Avenue, 59th Floor
New York, NY 10118
Website: www.av2books.com

Library of Congress Cataloging-in-Publication Data available upon request.
Fax 1-866-44-WEIGL for the attention of the Publishing Records department.

ISBN 978-1-4896-9733-2 (hardcover)
ISBN 978-1-4896-9734-9 (softcover)
ISBN 978-1-4896-9735-6 (multi-user eBook)
ISBN 978-1-4896-9736-3 (single-user eBook)

Printed in the United States of America in Brainerd, Minnesota
1 2 3 4 5 6 7 8 9 0 22 21 20 19 18

122018
102318

Project Coordinator: John Willis   Designer: Ana María Vidal

Every reasonable effort has been made to trace ownership and to obtain permission to reprint copyright material. The publishers would be pleased to have any errors or omissions brought to their attention so that they may be corrected in subsequent printings.

Weigl acknowledges Alamy, Dreamstime, Getty Images, iStock, Minden Pictures, NASA/Kenneth Cheung, Newscom, Shutterstock, and Wikimedia as its primary image suppliers for this title.

First published by North Star Editions in 2019

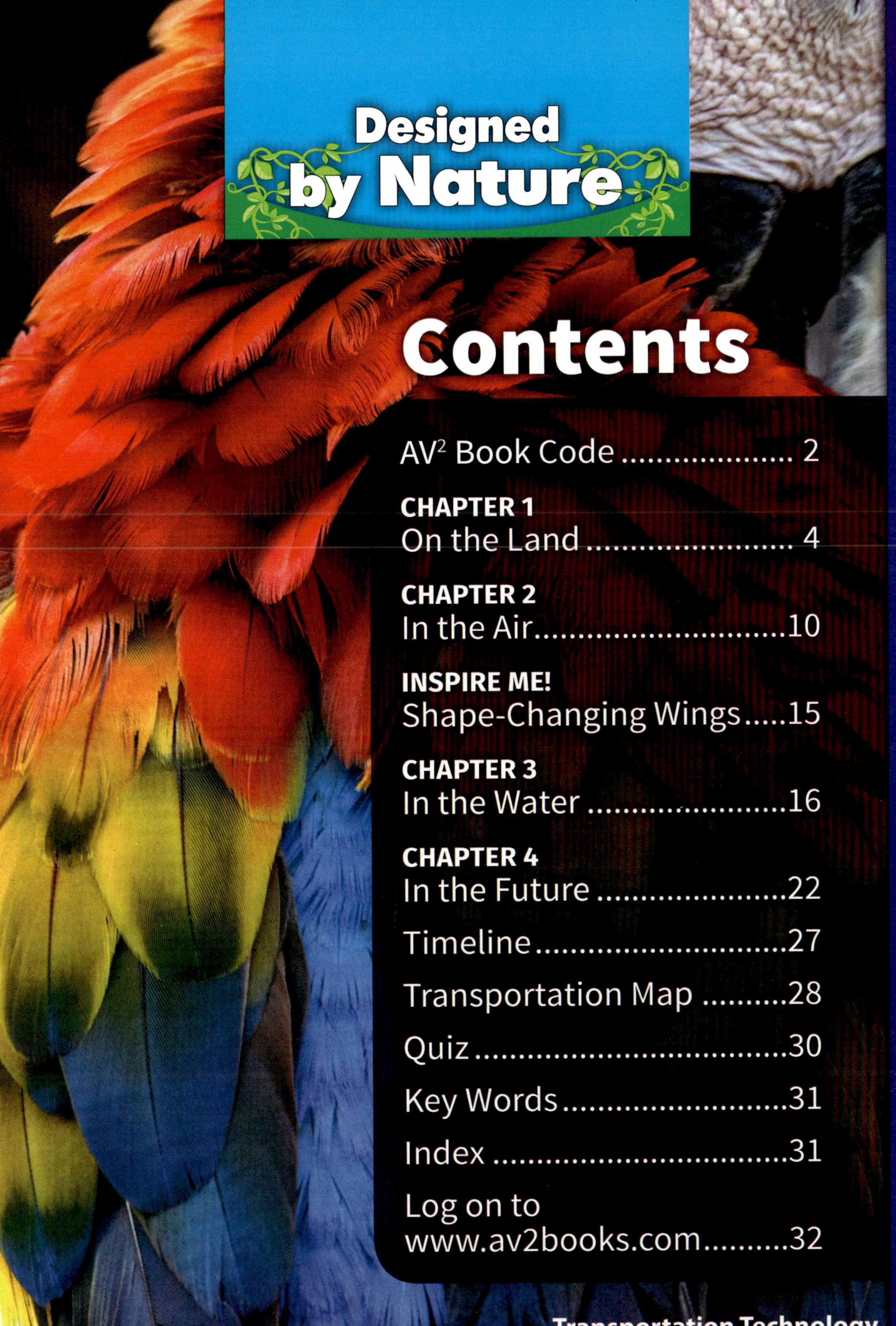

Contents

Chapter 1

In Japan, bullet trains carry travelers as fast as 199 miles per hour (320 kilometers per hour).

On the Land

Before modern transportation existed, people lived most of their lives in one small area. Today, many people travel all over the world. But moving from one place to another can be difficult. Scientists are always looking for faster and safer methods of travel.

Some of the best ideas for technology come from nature. Scientists have been inspired by nature for hundreds of years. They study nature to find ways to solve human problems. Then, they mimic nature's methods. This process is known as biomimicry.

The kingfisher uses its splash-less dive to sneak up on fish.

An example of biomimicry is the redesigned Shinkansen bullet train in Japan. Earlier bullet trains had flat noses that pushed a wall of air ahead of them. This created booming noises as the train entered tunnels. The noises were so loud that they damaged tunnels.

Engineers found a solution to the problem by watching kingfisher birds. The kingfisher dives into water without making a splash. The bird's long, narrow beak makes this possible. A rounded beak would push water forward. But the kingfisher's beak is pointed. As the bird dives, water flows smoothly past its beak.

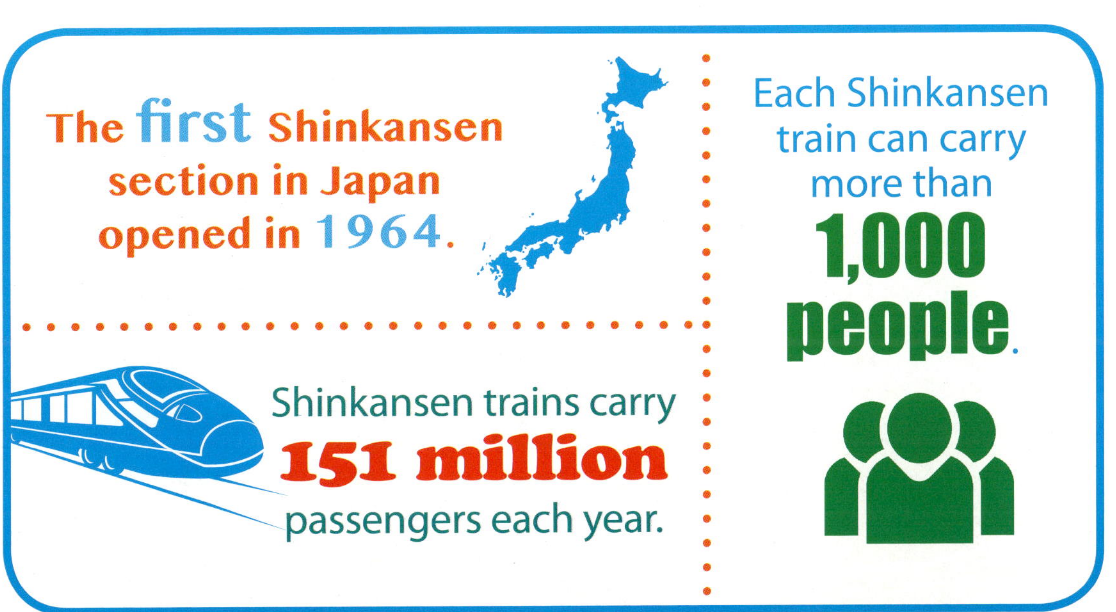

New bullet trains have a nose shaped like a kingfisher's beak. These trains are faster and quieter. They no longer create booming noises. Plus, they use up to 15 percent less energy.

Biomimicry has also led to many car designs. One example is the McLaren P1 car. This car was inspired by the sailfish. The sailfish is one of the fastest fish in the ocean. The force of water causes most fish to swim slower. But the sailfish's scales create small whirls of air. These pockets of air prevent water from touching the fish.

Designers created similar scales for the McLaren P1. They applied the scales to the **ducts** leading to the engine. The P1 engine is extremely powerful. It needs large amounts of air to burn fuel. Air also cools the engine. The scale-lined ducts feed more air into the engine. This increase in air makes the engine more **efficient**. Thanks to nature, cars can achieve more power using less energy.

The McLaren P1 is a hybrid car. It has both a gasoline engine and an electric motor.

Chapter 2

The long, stiff wing feathers that birds use to fly are known as flight feathers or remiges.

In the Air

Scientists dreamed of flying long before airplanes were invented. They studied birds to invent the first airplanes. Today, birds continue to inspire new aircraft.

In the 1970s, an engineer wanted to make airplanes more efficient. He looked to eagles for inspiration. Eagles curl the tips of their wings upward as they fly.

This helps them gain height. The engineer designed a vertical wing tip for airplanes. The wing tip, called a winglet, works similarly to an eagle's. The winglet makes it easier for the plane to cut through air. It also creates **lift**. As a result, the plane requires less fuel. Using less fuel also helps reduce air pollution. Today, most passenger planes have a form of winglets.

Planes with winglets tend to be quieter than planes without them.
norwegian.com

Aircraft often cause noise pollution. Noise pollution occurs when high levels of noise disturb human or animal life. Scientists want to make quieter airplanes. To learn how, they have looked to the owl.

Owls make very little noise when they fly. They have unique wings that reduce sound. Feathers at the front of the wing are shaped like a comb. As the owl flies, the edges of the feathers break up the flow of air. Feathers at the back of the wing have a **fringe**. This breaks up the air even more. The smaller masses of air create less noise. Owl feathers are also very soft. They absorb the sound made by the owl's wings.

Flying V

Large birds such as geese fly in the shape of a V. The birds in the front create whirling masses of air. The masses of air help lift the birds in the back. This allows the birds to use less energy. Military pilots use the same shape when flying in a group. This way, they use less fuel.

Scientists hope to add similar designs to airplanes. They designed an aircraft propeller blade with a comb-like edge. The blade mimics an owl's front wing feathers. Owls have inspired other ideas, too. One is a fringe that attaches to airplane wings. Another is a coating for the plane's landing gear. The coating would mimic the texture of owl feathers.

The leading edge of an owl feather has a comb-like pattern. The trailing edge has a fringe.

Inspire Me!

Shape-Changing Wings

Birds can adjust the amount their feathers overlap. This changes the shapes of their wings. Birds use different wing shapes as they fly. For instance, they make their wings long when they turn. To fly faster, they make their wings short. A shorter wing helps reduce **drag**.

Scientists hope to use shape-changing wings on airplanes. They are designing a wing made of many parts. These tiny, lightweight parts can form different shapes as the plane flies. As a result, the wings can bend and twist. The parts are covered in strips of a flexible material. The strips mimic bird feathers. They move across one another as the wing changes shape. The strips create a smooth wing surface.

Shape-changing wings allow planes to move more easily through the air. They are also lighter than other wings. Therefore, the plane uses less energy as it flies. This saves fuel.

A shape-changing wing is less rigid than other wings.

Chapter 3

Sharks swim in short bursts of speed when chasing after prey.

In the Water

The way animals move through water has always fascinated scientists. Many scientists study sea animals to learn from their movements. This gives them ideas for new transportation technology.

Sharks are fast swimmers. Scientists studied sharkskin to find out why. The skin is lined with small, tooth-like scales. These structures are called denticles. As a shark swims, the denticles direct water over the shark's body. This allows for swift, easy movement. It also keeps tiny sea creatures from attaching to the shark's body. Thanks to their denticles, sharks have few to no **parasites**.

Scientists made a material that mimics sharkskin. It uses the same pattern of small structures. The material can be used on boats and airplanes. It keeps algae from attaching to boats. It also reduces drag and saves energy. The material could be used on many surfaces to resist **bacteria**.

Smooth Swimming

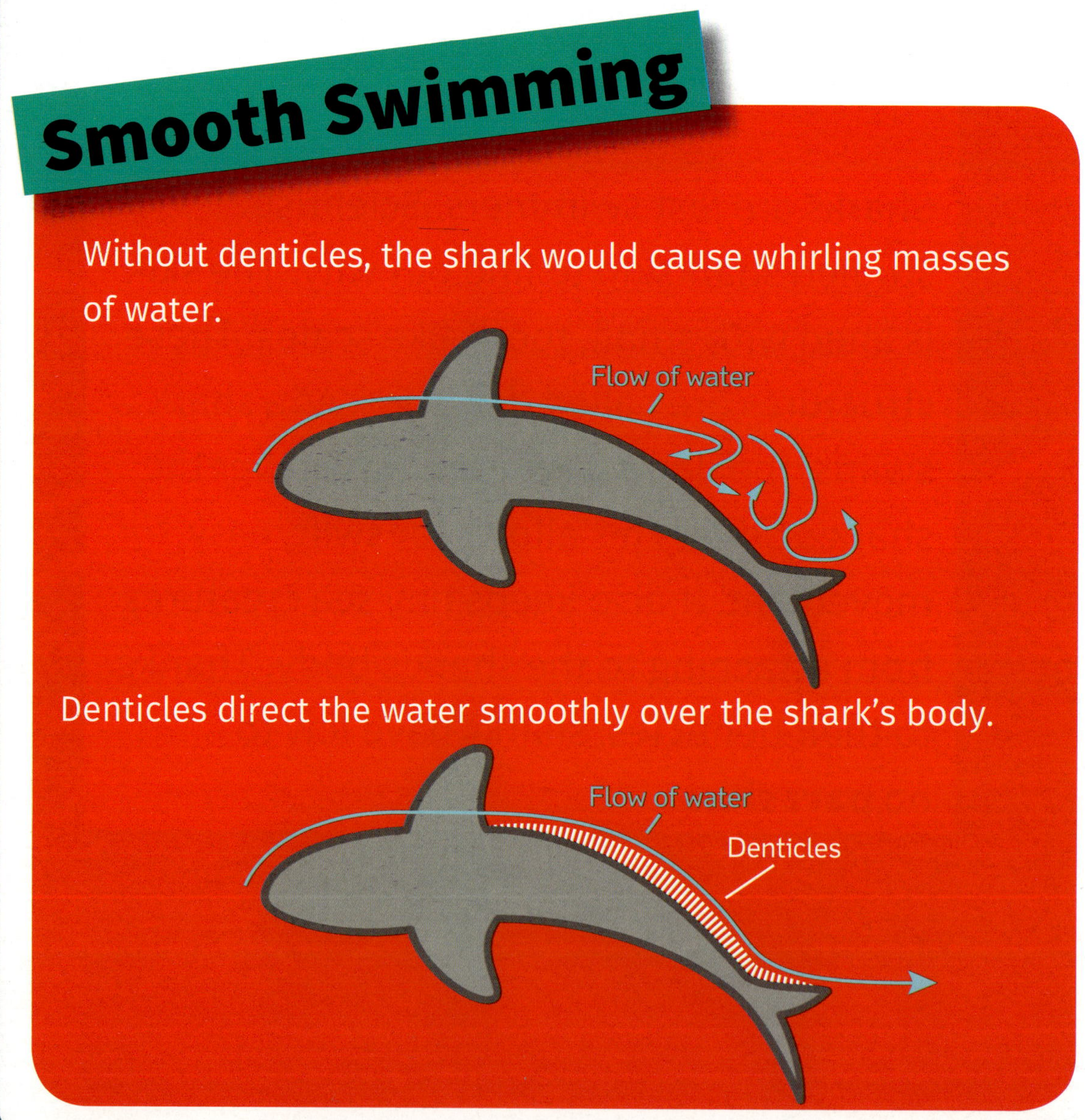

Octopuses have inspired scientists as well. These animals are skilled at escaping predators. An octopus swims headfirst away from danger. To swim, the octopus takes water into its body. Then, it squirts the water out through a funnel. This is a tube-shaped organ near the octopus's head. The force of the water pushes the octopus forward. The octopus changes direction by turning the funnel.

Scientists have created a similar system for boats. Four balloon-like containers attach to the boat. These containers take in water. Then, a cable around the containers squeezes the water out. This makes the boat move. The new system can be used on a variety of small watercraft. The containers are quieter than boat propellers. They are also safer. Fish cannot get caught in them.

A Whale of a Sub

Killer whales are some of the fastest animals in the ocean. One company sells a submarine inspired by killer whales. The submarine can take two people approximately 5 feet (1.5 m) underwater. It can move up to 50 miles per hour (81 km/h). It can even jump out of the water, similar to a whale. The submarine's fins make these movements possible. The pilot uses levers and foot pedals to control the fins.

An octopus can briefly move at speeds of up to 25 miles per hour (40 kilometers per hour) when swimming.

Chapter 4

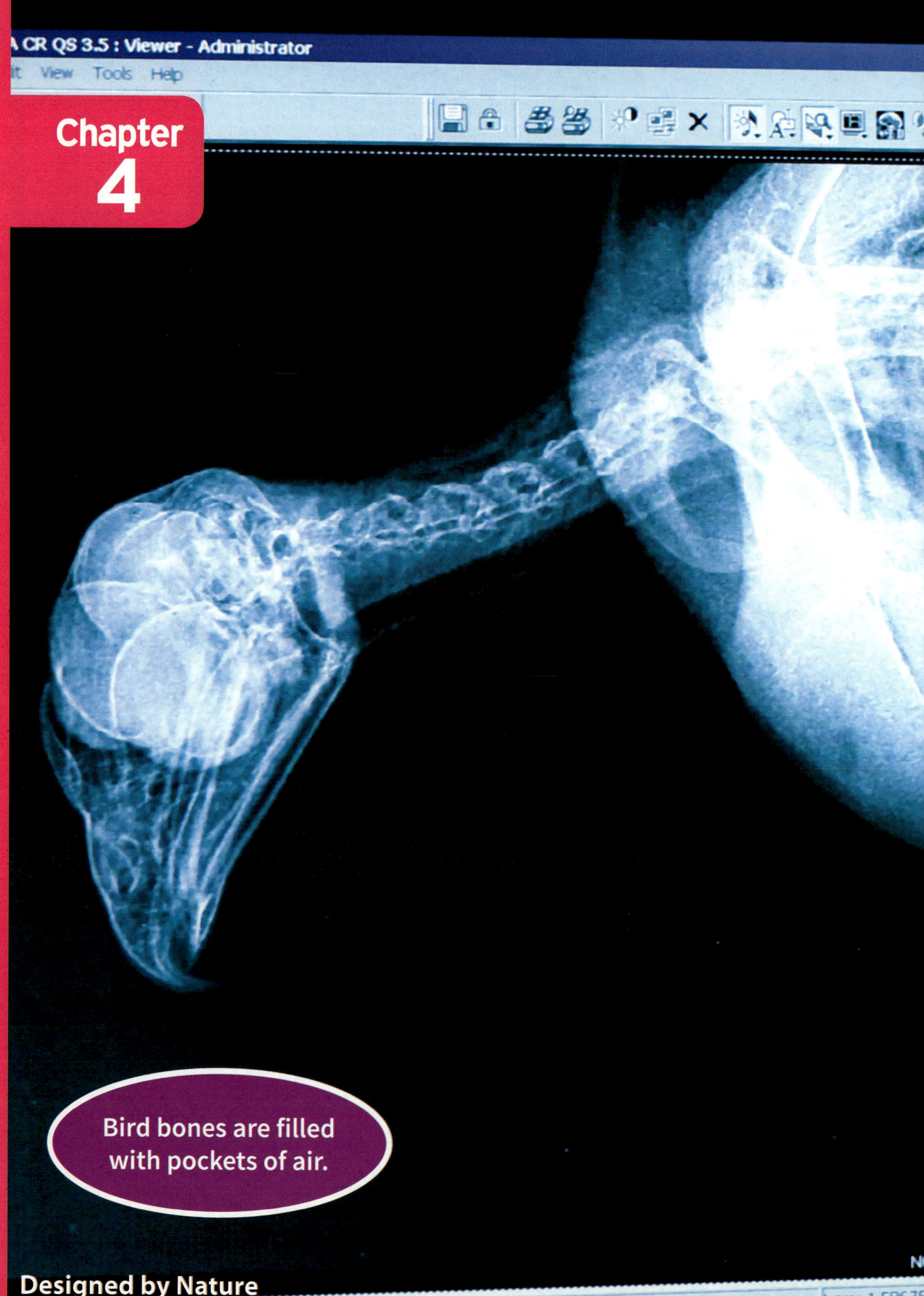

Bird bones are filled with pockets of air.

In the Future

Transportation technology is always changing. Nature has inspired many of today's transportation methods. Now, nature is paving the way for designs of the future.

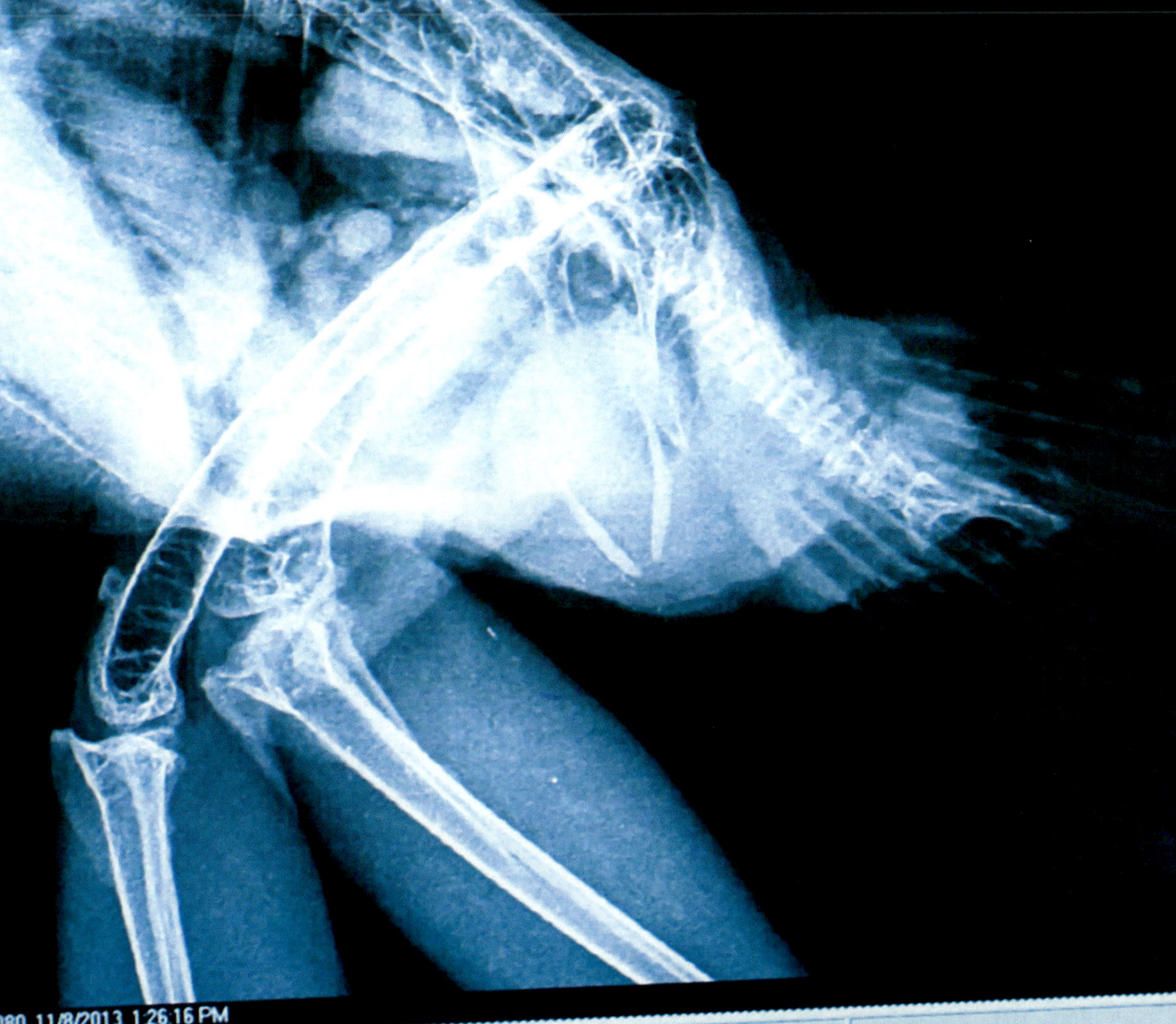

Car sensors may use cameras, radar, or ultrasonic waves.

One airplane company is designing a see-through plane. The plane's body is similar to the bone structure of birds. Bird bones are mostly hollow. Inside the bone, thin walls cross one another to make a web-like pattern. This makes the bones light but strong. The see-through plane will have a web of support beams. The beams provide strength only where necessary. This allows for more space between the beams. Large windows will fill the extra space. That way, people can see out and above the plane as they fly.

Nature is also inspiring future car designs. Engineers want to do a better job of preventing car crashes. They are studying how fish move. Fish swim in large groups called schools. However, they never run into one another. Each fish adjusts its speed to match the speed of other fish.

Atlantic herring can form groups with hundreds of millions of fish.

Schools of fish **self-organize**. They do not have leaders.

80 percent of fish live in schools at some point during their lives.

Many new cars have a similar feature. The cars contain devices called sensors. The sensors measure the speeds of other cars. They can tell if other cars are nearby. The car uses this information to avoid crashing. It can speed up or slow down without direction from the driver. Some cars can automatically stop to avoid a crash.

Humans make many mistakes while driving. Driverless cars would use computers to remove error. These cars would have fish-like instincts. With fewer errors, humans could travel more safely.

A Mobile Ant

In 2013, car designers took part in a design challenge. They designed cars using biomimicry. One group of designers came up with a car called the Mobilliant. The design is modeled after an ant. An ant takes in oxygen and other gases through its **exoskeleton**. The Mobilliant would take in gases through its lid. Then, it would turn the gases into **fertilizer**. The car would also have two tanks. This is similar to ants, which have two stomachs. The Mobilliant could even climb walls.

Timeline

Since first observing birds in the air, people have been inspired by movement in nature. Today, the technology exists to make many of these concepts a reality.

1505 Italian inventor Leonardo da Vinci writes his *Codex on the Flight of Birds*. This document proposes ideas for bird-based flying machines.

1903 The Wright brothers make the first flight using a powered aircraft. Its wings, like those of a bird, change shape to allow it to turn.

1973 After an embargo causes aircraft fuel prices to increase, engineer Richard T. Whitcomb designs winglets based on eagle wings to improve the efficiency of airplanes.

1997 Engineers from the West Japan Railway company create new bullet trains based on kingfisher beaks. These new trains are up to 10 percent faster.

2013 Scientists at Brown University use 3D printers to create **artificial** bat wings. By examining these artificial wings, they hope to use them in small aircraft.

2016 At a motor show in Geneva, Switzerland, one automobile company reveals a concept for a sphere-shaped tire with tread patterns based on brain coral.

Transportation Map

Pacific Ocean

North America

Atlantic Ocean

South America

People have turned to nature for transportation for centuries. Today, scientists around the world are working to develop newer, more efficient methods of moving people from place to place.

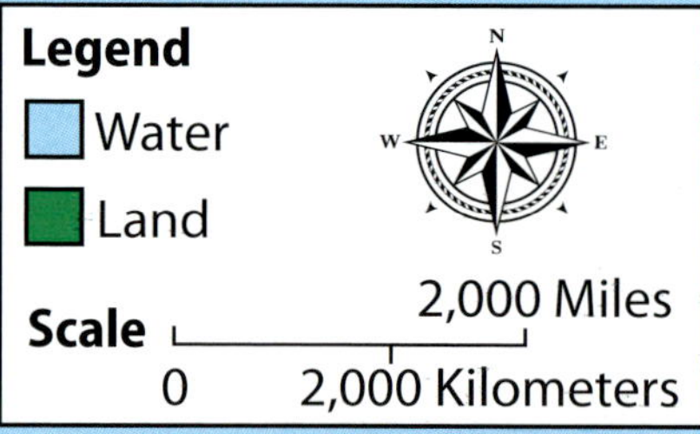

United States

At the Worcester Polytechnic Institute of Massachusetts, scientists examined how bumblebees communicate with each other. Using this data, they can help wirelessly connected vehicles track each other.

Great Britain

In 2014, McLaren Automotive, in Woking, Great Britain, developed the sailfish-based McLaren P1 supercar. Its fish-inspired design increased efficiency by 17 percent.

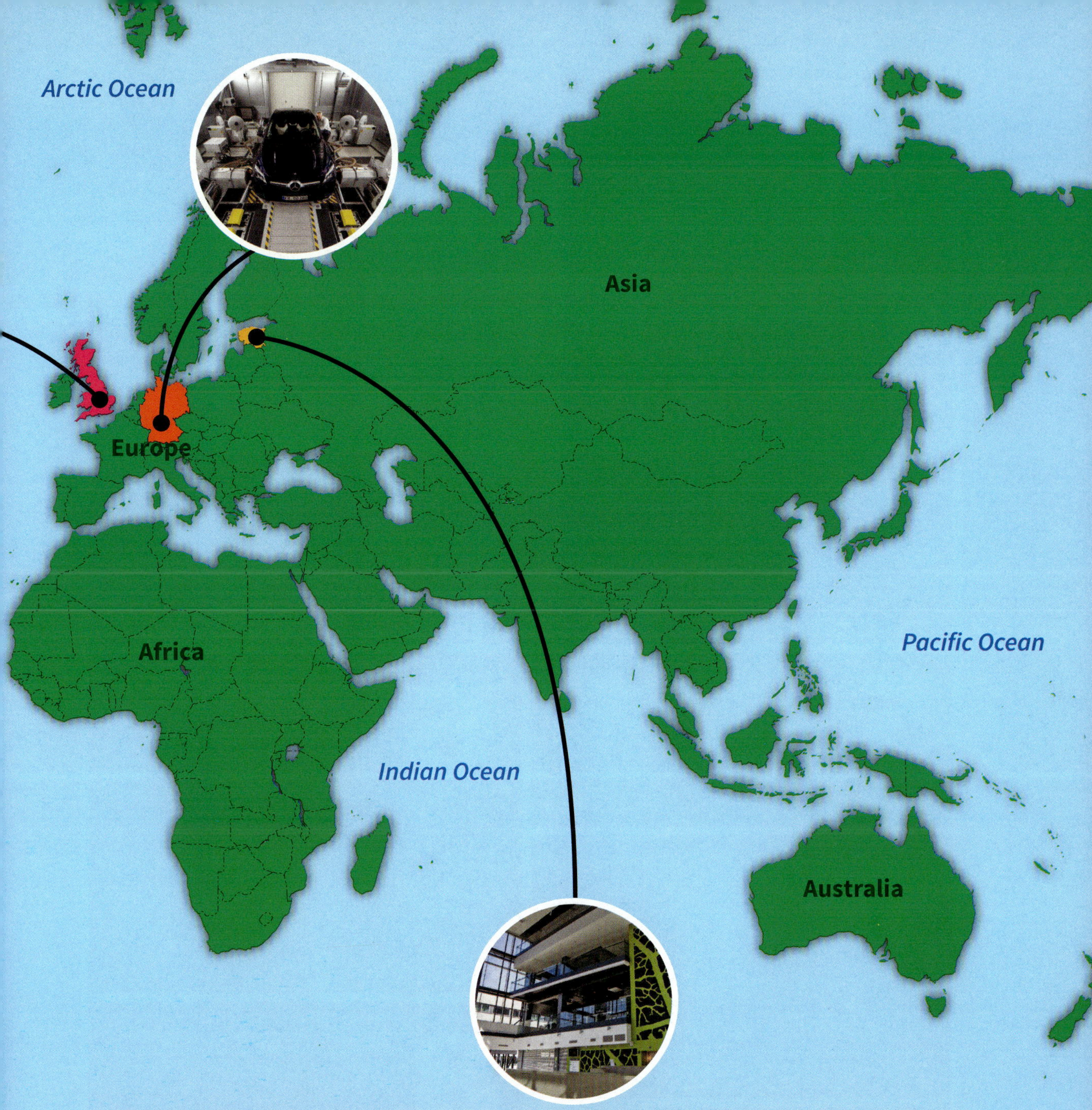

Germany

Designers at the Mercedes Technology Center, in Sindelfingen, Germany, developed a concept car in 2005 that was based on a boxfish. The car's shape balanced streamlined features with the need to hold passengers.

Estonia

Researchers at the Tallinn University of Technology in Tallinn, Estonia, developed a new method of underwater propulsion based on sea turtle flippers in 2013. They plan on using it to make swimming robots.

Quiz

1 Do schools of fish have leaders?

Answer: No

2 When was the first human flight that used a powered aircraft?

Answer: 1903

3 What is a denticle?

Answer: A tooth-like scale on a shark's body

4 What is the vertical wing tip used on airplanes called?

Answer: A winglet

5 What animal inspired the noses of Japan's bullet trains?

Answer: A kingfisher

6 Where is an octopus's funnel?

Answer: Slightly below its eye

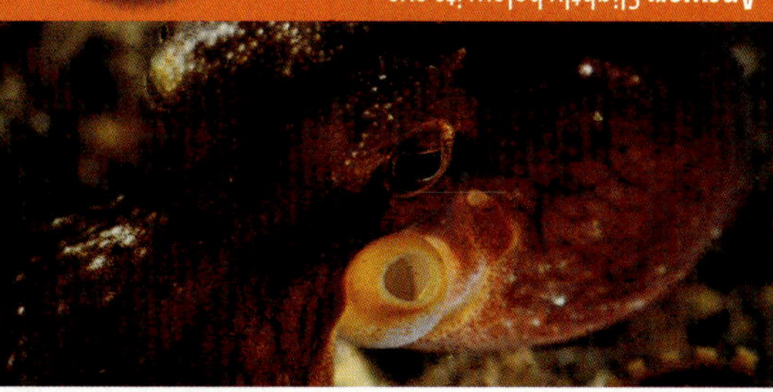

7 Which university had researchers develop a method of underwater propulsion based on sea turtle flippers?

Answer: Tallinn University of Technology, in Estonia

8 What are bird bones filled with?

Answer: Hollow pockets of air

9 Which birds are known for their quiet flights?

Answer: Owls

10 What animal inspired the McLaren P1?

Answer: The sailfish

Key Words

artificial: made by humans instead of occurring naturally

bacteria: single-celled living things. They can be useful or harmful.

drag: the force of air pushing back against a moving object

ducts: tubes used to carry air

efficient: accomplishing as much as possible with as little effort or resources as possible

exoskeleton: a skeleton outside the body. An exoskeleton supports and protects an animal's body.

fertilizer: a substance that helps plants grow

fringe: a border of loose or hanging material in the shape of strips or strings

lift: upward movement

parasites: animals or plants that live on or in other living things

Index

Log on to www.av2books.com

AV² by Weigl brings you media enhanced books that support active learning. Go to www.av2books.com, and enter the special code found on page 2 of this book. You will gain access to enriched and enhanced content that supplements and complements this book. Content includes video, audio, weblinks, quizzes, a slide show, and activities.

AV² Online Navigation

Audio
Listen to sections of the book read aloud.

Book Pages
AV² pages directly correspond to pages in the book.

Video
Watch informative video clips.

Embedded Weblinks
Gain additional information for research.

Key Words
Study vocabulary, and complete a matching word activity.

Try This!
Complete activities and hands-on experiments.

Quizzes
Test your knowledge.

Slide Show
View images and captions, and prepare a presentation.

AV² was built to bridge the gap between print and digital. We encourage you to tell us what you like and what you want to see in the future.

Sign up to be an AV² Ambassador at www.av2books.com/ambassador.

Due to the dynamic nature of the Internet, some of the URLs and activities provided as part of AV² by Weigl may have changed or ceased to exist. AV² by Weigl accepts no responsibility for any such changes. All media enhanced books are regularly monitored to update addresses and sites in a timely manner. Contact AV² by Weigl at 1-866-649-3445 or av2books@weigl.com with any questions, comments, or feedback.